Made in the USA
Coppell, TX
13 January 2021

48161016R00056